JOHN HARBISON

MILOSZ SONGS

FOR VOICE AND PIANO

Poems by
Czeslaw Milosz

duration ca. 17 minutes

AMP 8234
First Printing: November 2008

ISBN: 978-1-4234-5899-9

Associated Music Publishers, Inc.

DISTRIBUTED BY
HAL•LEONARD®
CORPORATION
7777 W. BLUEMOUND RD. P.O. BOX 13819 MILWAUKEE, WI 53213

Commissioned by the New York Philharmonic
Lorin Maazel, Music Director.

The first performance of MILOSZ SONGS was given on 23 February 2006
by Dawn Upshaw with the New York Philharmonic
conducted by Robert Spano.

The version of MILOSZ SONGS for voice and piano
was first performed by Emily Hindrichs, soprano
and Brett Hodgdon, piano on 15 April 2008
at New England Conservatory's Jordon Hall.

Performance material including the vocal score to the complete set of songs written
for soprano and orchestra may be obtained on loan from the publisher.
G. Schirmer and Associated Music Publishers Rental Department
P.O. Box 572
445 Bellvale Road
Chester, NY 10918
(845) 469-4699
(845) 469-7544 (fax)

Program Note
to accompany the original orchestral version

Milosz Songs was commissioned by the New York Philharmonic for performance by Dawn Upshaw – my first piece for the orchestra, my fourth for her. Writing for Dawn Upshaw has always encouraged me to try new things. This piece surrounds the singer with a *concertino* group of six players: three flutes, vibraphone, harp, and celeste. This *concertino* plays an important, varied role in every song. I thought of these players as satellites revolving around the path of the singer.

Milosz's poems are Epilogues for the twentieth century. He was witness to its most harrowing events. He draws us, unready, as he was, into the great sweep of that history. Always, he reacts, as in "Encounter," "not out of sorrow, but in wonder."

As a *reader* I return again and again to such fierce, cunning, sweeping mid-length poems as "Preparation," "Ars Poetica?," "No More," "Counsels." As a *composer* I am drawn to fragmentary short lyrics, grateful for their elusive melody, their barely reconciled dissonant elements, their embrace of the every day.

In 1994, I made my first Milosz setting, "December 1" (part of *Flashes and Illuminations* for baritone and piano). That poem concludes:

I describe this for I have learned to doubt philosophy:
and the visible world is all that remains.

Czeslaw Milosz was born in Szetejnie, Lithuania in 1911. He was part of the Polish Resistance movement during World War II, and was the cultural attachée with the Polish Embassy in Paris. He defected to France in 1951. From 1960 to 1999 he taught at the University of California, Berkeley.

Milosz received the Nobel Prize for literature in 1980. He died in Krakow in January 2004.

During his half-century in the U.S., Milosz became involved in the translation of his poems. Working with students and colleagues, as well as by himself, he produced vivid English versions.

I am grateful to Harper Collins Books for permission to use these translations from the Polish originals.

—John Harbison

Information on John Harbison and his works is available at www.schirmer.com

MILOSZ SONGS

Prologue: from **Lauda**

And now we are joined in a ritual.
In amber? In crystal? We make music.
Neither what once was nor what ever will be.
Only what persists when the world is over.

What Once Was Great

What once was great, now appeared small.
Kingdoms were fading like snow-covered bronze.

What once could smite, now smites no more.
Celestial earths roll on and shine.

Stretched on the grass by the bank of a river,
As long, long ago, I launch my boats of bark.

Montgeron, 1959

So Little

I said so little.
Days were short.

Short days.
Short nights.
Short years.

I said so little.
I couldn't keep up.

My heart grew weary
From joy,
Despair,
Ardor,
Hope.

The jaws of Leviathan
Were closing upon me.

Naked, I lay on the shores
Of desert islands.

The white whale of the world
Hauled me down to its pit.

And now I don't know
What in all that was real.

Berkeley, 1969

When the Moon

When the moon rises and women in flowery
dresses are strolling,
I am struck by their eyes, eyelashes, and the whole
arrangement of the world.
It seems to me that from such a strong mutual
attraction
The ultimate truth should issue at last.

Berkeley, 1966

On Old Women

Invisible, dressed in clothes too big for me,
I take a walk, pretending I am a detached mind.

What country is this? Funereal wreaths, devalued medals,
a general avoidance of remembering what happened.

I think of you, old women, silently fingering past days
of your lives like the beads of your rosaries.

It had to be suffered, endured, managed.
One had to wait and not wait, one had to.

I send my prayers for you to the Highest, helped
by your faces in old photographs.

May the day of your death not be a day of hopelessness,
but of trust in the light that shines through earthly forms.

Epilogue: from **Winter**

And now I am ready to keep running
When the sun rises beyond the borderlands of death.

I already see mountain ridges in the heavenly forest
Where, beyond every essence, a new essence waits.

You, music of my late years, I am called
By a sound and a color which are more and more perfect.

Do not die out, fire.
Enter my dreams, love.
Be young forever, seasons of the earth.

Post-Epilogue: **Rays of Dazzling Light**

Light off metal shaken,
Lucid dew of heaven,
Bless each and every one
To whom the earth is given.

Its essence was always hidden
Behind a distant curtain.
We chased it all our lives
Bidden and unbidden.

Knowing the hunt would end,
That then what had been rent
Would be at last made whole:
Poor body and the soul.

MILOSZ SONGS for Soprano and Orchestra

Instrumentation

3 Flutes (2nd doubling Piccolo, 3rd doubling Alto Flute)
2 Oboes (2nd doubling English Horn)
2 Clarinets in B flat (2nd doubling Bass Clarinet)
2 Bassoons (2nd doubling Contrabassoon)

2 Horns in F
2 Trumpets in C
Trombone
Bass Trombone

Timpani
Percussion (3 Players)
Vibraphone, Marimba, Temple Blocks, 3 Triangles, Crotales (Eb),
2 Tuned Gongs (Bb, B), Tubular Bell (D), Tamtam, Crash Cymbal,
Suspended Cymbal, Snare Drum, Bass Drum, Tambourine

Celesta
Harp

Solo Soprano

Strings (10.10.8.6.4 maximum)

duration ca. 30 minutes

Prologue: from *Lauda*
*A Task
*Encounter
*You Who Wronged
When the Moon
*O!
What Once Was Great
So Little
On Old Women
Epilogue: from *Winter*
Post-Epilogue: *Rays of Dazzling Light*

These songs are not included in the published version for voice and piano.

MILOSZ SONGS
(for voice and piano)
Prologue: from *Lauda*

Czeslaw Milosz

John Harbison

once was＿ nor what ev - er will be.＿

On - ly what per - sists when the

world is o - ver.

What Once Was Great

bronze. _____

What once ____ could smite, ____ now smites no more. _____

Ce - les - tial earths roll on

and shine.

Tempo I

Stretched on the grass by the bank of a ri - ver,

As long, _____ long a - go, _____

I launch _____ my boats of

bark. _____

So Little

Allegro con fuoco
♩ = 160

I said so lit-tle. Days were short.

Short days. Short nights. Short years. ____

white whale   of the world _____   Hauled   me   down   to   its

pit.

And now   I don't know,   and   now   I don't   know   What   in   all

When the Moon

should is — — — — — sue at

last

rit.

On Old Women

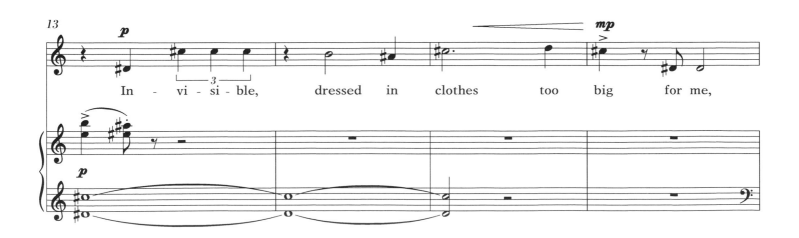

In - vi - si - ble, dressed in clothes too big for me,

I take a walk, pre-tend-ing I ___ am a de-tached mind. ___

parlando, agitato

What coun-try is this?

Fu - ne - re-al wreaths

animando

de - val - ued ___ me - dals, ___ a gen-er-al a - voi - dance of re-

Epilogue: from *Winter*

Lento, sognando

♩ = 66

And now __ I am rea-dy to keep run-ning __ When
the sun ris - es be - yond __ the bor - der-lands of death.
I al - rea - dy see _____ moun-tain rid - ges in the hea - ven - ly for-est
Where, be - yond ev - ery es - sence, a new __ es - sence __

Post-Epilogue: *Rays of Dazzling Light*

Tempo Giusto ♩ = 108